This book is one of a series designed for young toddlers who are beginning to talk and to put names to things which they see around them. Clear, colourful illustrations with a single label depict things which are either very familiar or which will provide a learning situation.

The contemporary nature of the objects will ensure recognition by the child. The adult will also be able to talk around the subject, making it relevant to the child's own environment.

Happy first birthday

Lots of love

from

Calum McDoug
xx

First picture book
Toys

illustrated by
PETER LONGDEN

Ladybird Books   Loughborough

teddy bear

rabbit

5

puppets

rag doll

jigsaw

bricks

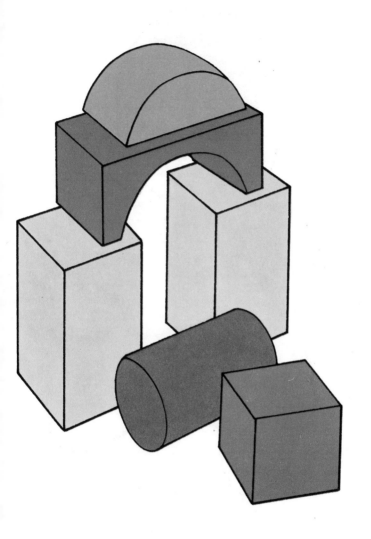

doll

Action Man

boat

duck

rattle

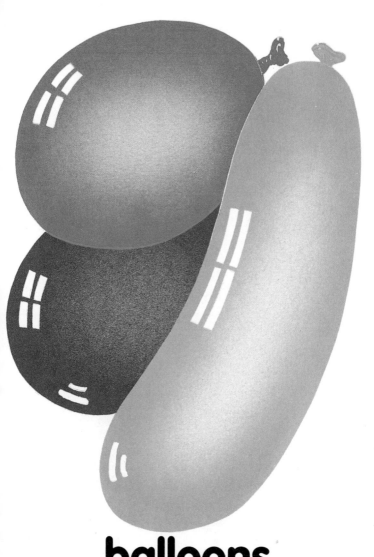

balloons

jack-in-a-box

musical toy

building bricks

21

basket

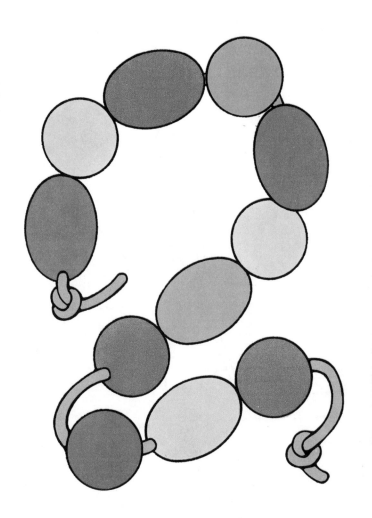

beads

bubbles

24

top

tricycle

car

doll's pram

wheelbarrow

trolley

WELL-LOVED
TALES

The Town Mouse
and the
Country Mouse

book

dog

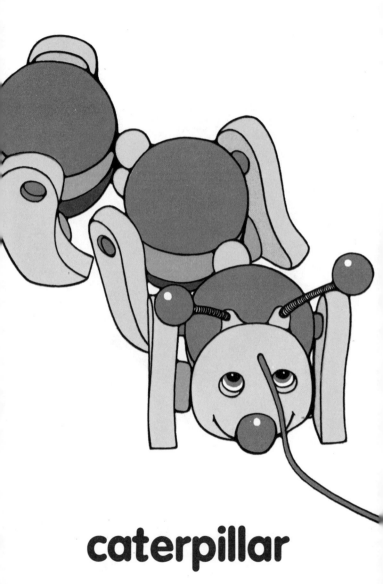

caterpillar

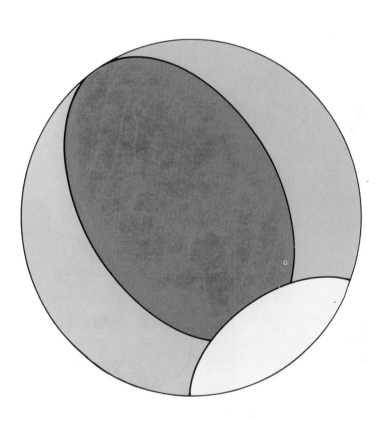

ball

skittles

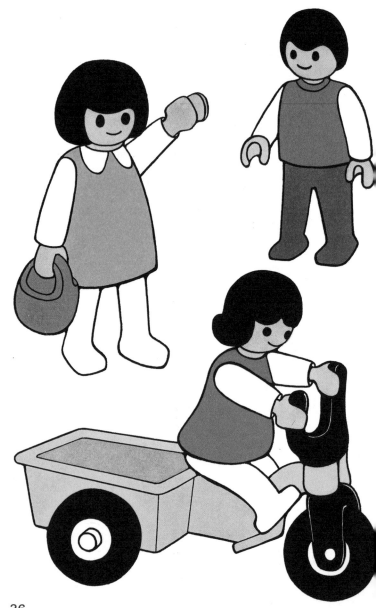

toy people

engine

plane

helicopter

telephone

rocking horse

43

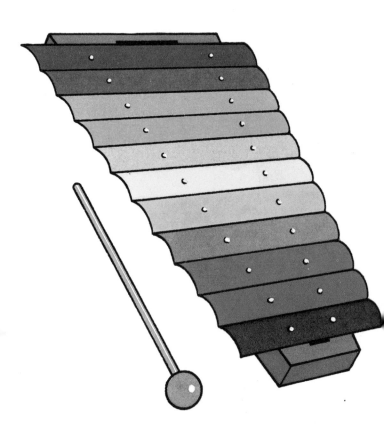

xylophone

drum

bucket and spade

paddling pool

swing

slide

games